SUPER HEROES

Written by: Kenji L. Jackson

With: Heddrick McBride

Illustrated by: HH-Pax

Dedication:

This book is dedicated to the many police officers, teachers, firefighters and coaches who are committed to making a difference in and around the communities you serve. Your hard work, sacrifice and impact especially on our youth is greatly appreciated. You are true Super Heroes!

I want to thank my parents, siblings, family, closest friends, Morgan State University and The Men of TTC for your love and for continuing to support the Bringing Kids Success Mission. Most of all I want to thank my son Kaiden Li for being the greatest gift a father could ask for. Daddy loves you!

Police officers are important to your city and important to your community.

They work really hard to keep you safe and teach love, peace and unity.

You should not feel afraid of the Police because they are there for your protection.

If you are lost and feel helpless, the police can point you in the right direction.

Police officers do many different things to be of service in and around town.

They help with traffic, patrol neighborhoods and try to keep crime down.

Police officers can be found at the mall, at the park, in the bank and airport.

They are also seen at the train station, in school, in stadiums and in court.

When police officers have free time, they can be seen playing with kids and having fun.

They play basketball, football, and jumping rope whether it's cold or in the sun.

Police officers are expected to protect and serve us all, and be proud to wear blue.

Being a police officer is an important job and you can become a police officer too!

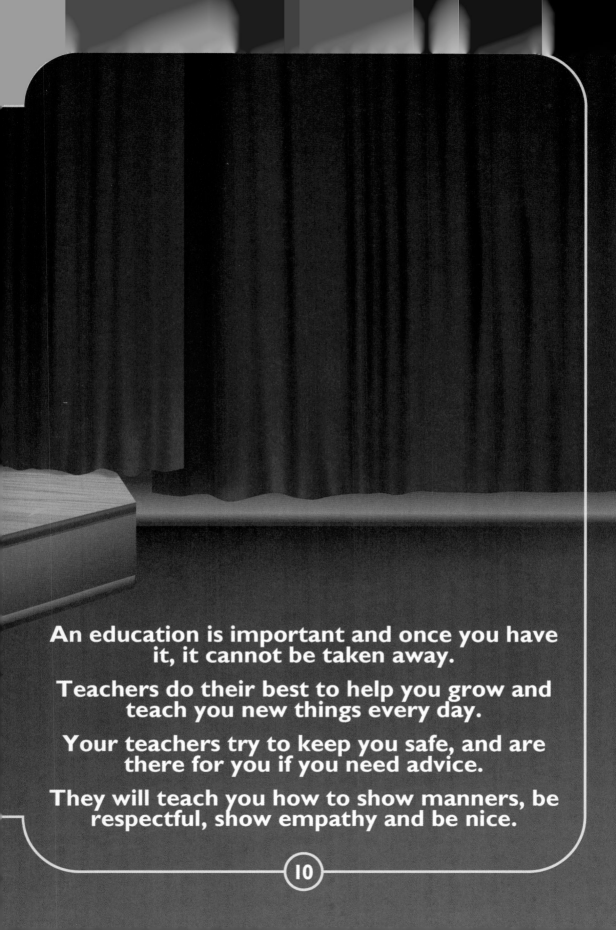

An education is important and once you have it, it cannot be taken away.

Teachers do their best to help you grow and teach you new things every day.

Your teachers try to keep you safe, and are there for you if you need advice.

They will teach you how to show manners, be respectful, show empathy and be nice.

If you need help with your school work, teachers are there to lend a helping hand.

Teachers will teach you study skills and show you how to take notes and plan.

Teachers are willing to stay after to school with you so you can improve your grades.

They teach you important lessons about life and prepare you for different careers and trades.

Teachers work with your parents to support you as you continue to learn and grow.

They give you the self-confidence to be proud and to show off all the things you know.

Teachers even come to your games and performances and congratulate you on a job well done.

Teachers are important to your community and when you grow up maybe you will become one!

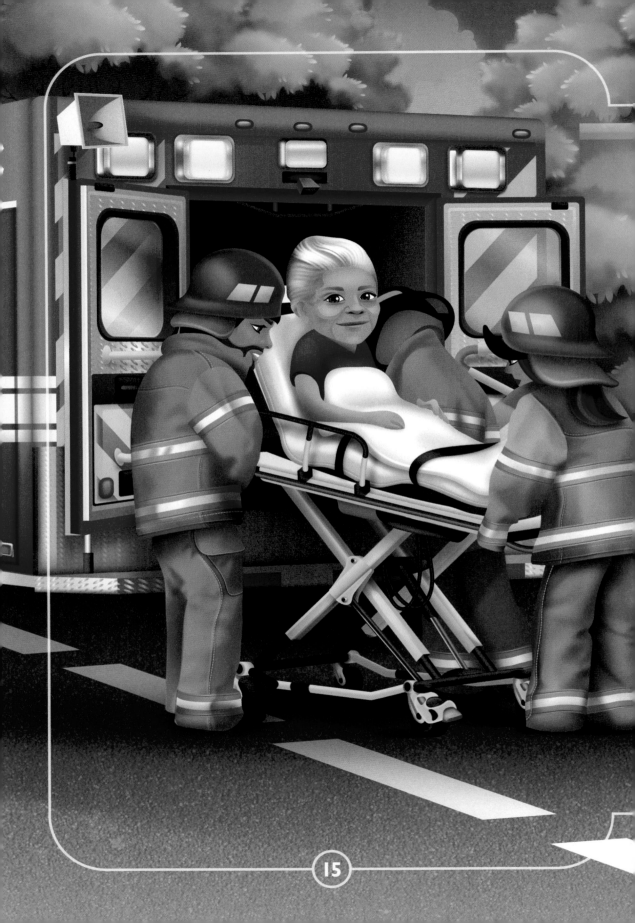

Fire fighters are very important to your community
and they try to keep people safe from harm.

Fire fighters work in fire stations and are ready to
help people in need at the sound of an alarm.

Putting out dangerous fires is not the only thing fire
fighters do to save lives by far.

Fire fighters respond to emergency calls just like
paramedics and are trained in CPR.

Fire fighters are able to get to people in need of help and take them to the hospital for care.

Fire truck sirens can be heard to clear the way when Fire fighters are trying to get somewhere.

Fire fighters have to stay in shape and have strength to carry heavy things like a fire hose.

Sometimes they have to climb a lot of stairs while wearing heavy protective clothes.

Fire truck

Fire fighters can be seen in schools teaching kids about safety and practicing fire drills.

To be a Fire fighter you have to be smart and brave and learn a lot of skills.

Fire stations can be found in places like cities, towns and even in your neighborhood.

Firefighters are important to us all and if you became a firefighter that would be good!

Coaches help you in the gym and on the field but to them there is more than just sports.

Coaches want to help you become a good all-around person and are there for extra support.

Being a good student and athlete are sure to make your coaches proud.

They will encourage you to be your own person and to never follow the wrong crowd.

To some kids around the world, a coach is all they have to be there for them in times of need.

Coaches help with homework and studying and also build your strength and speed.

Teamwork, responsibility and leadership are important lessons coaches want you to learn.

Coaches set high expectations and teach you that everything you want you have to earn.

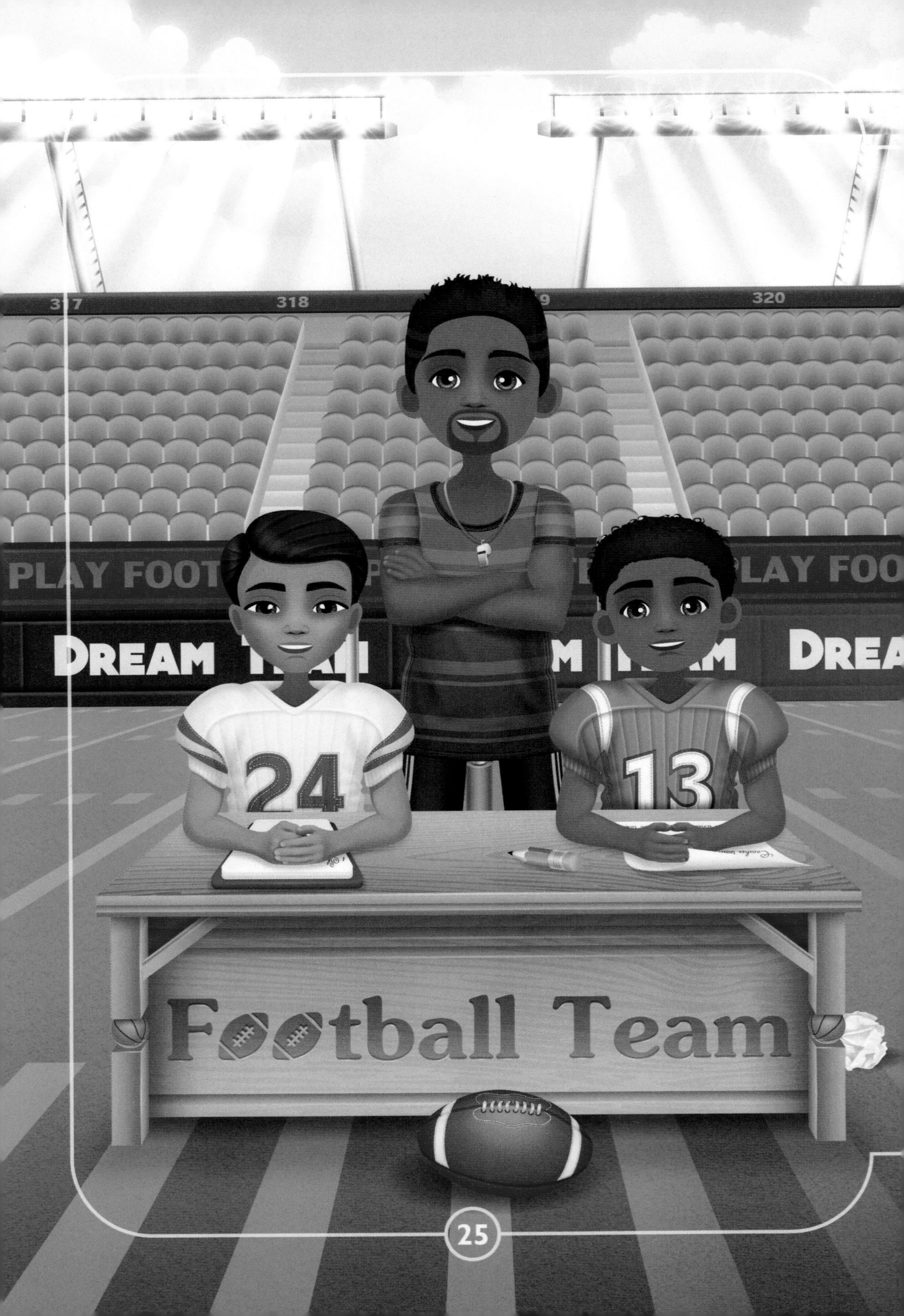
PLAY FOOT
DREAM TEAM
PLAY FOO
DREA
24
13
Football Team

316 317 318 319

···PLAY FOOTBALL··· PLAY FOOTBALL··· PLAY FO

EAM | DREAM TEAM | DREAM TEAM | D

Coaches teach you how to be a good sport and to show high character whether you win or lose.

Coaches will prepare you to be successful no matter what sport or activity you choose.

Coaches work with you to get you ready for college and can help you get into a great school.

Coaches are very important to your community and being a coach is really cool!

VISIT
www.bksworldwide .net
FOR MORE TITLES

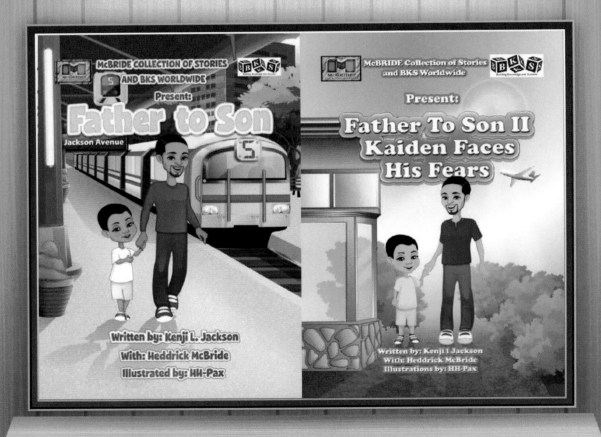

Made in the USA
Monee, IL
18 January 2020